REVELATION AND TRADITION

Holy Trinity Abbey
Huntsville, Utah.
Feb. 10, 1970

S0-ATT-599

ABOUT THE BOOK

The relation between revelation and tradition, which has been a crucial issue in Catholic theology, particularly since the Modernist crisis, has been clarified by the Constitution *De revelatione* of the Second Vatican Council. In the present work, Karl Rahner and Joseph Ratzinger, both Council periti, explore some of the speculative and historical foundations of the Constitution. For Rahner, revelation is the act whereby man's transcendent vocation to the supernatural is made clearly manifest by God in concrete historical events. The medium of this manifestation is the believer's response—whether explicit or not—to the Word incarnate in history and to the Spirit who acts pre-eminently through the historical reality of the Church. Thus is sketched a radically fresh approach to understanding the nature of salvation history in its relation to the life of the Trinity, to "secular" history, and to the history of religions in general. Joseph Ratzinger provides a historical corollary to Rahner's conclusions by a detailed appraisal of the arguments set forth at the Council of Trent in answer to the Reformers' emphasis on *sola scriptura*. Moving away from the thesis of J. R. Geiselmann, Ratzinger shows that while the Bible retains its central place in Christian belief, the concept of tradition implied by Trent nevertheless embraces more than merely the notion of the transmission of the scriptures. Tradition in its deepest sense is the Church's living consciousness of its faith in the revealing Word, and as such is the hermeneutical key to grasping the written word of the Bible.

QUAESTIONES DISPUTATAE

KARL RAHNER
JOSEPH RATZINGER

REVELATION
AND
TRADITION

HERDER AND HERDER

1966
HERDER AND HERDER NEW YORK
232 Madison Avenue, New York, N.Y. 10016

Original edition, "Offenbarung und Überlieferung",
Herder, Freiburg, 1965
Translated by W. J. O'HARA

Nihil Obstat: Hubertus J. Richards, S.T.L., L.S.S.
Censor deputatus

Imprimatur: ✠ Patritius Casey, Vic. Gen.

Westmonasterii, die 7a Martii, 1966

The Nihil Obstat and Imprimatur are a declaration that a book or pamphlet
is considered to be free from doctrinal or moral error.

It is not implied that those who have granted the Nihil Obstat and Imprimatur agree
with the contents, opinions or statements expressed.

Library of Congress Catalog Card Number: 66–18747
First published in West Germany © 1966 Herder KG
Printed in the Republic of Ireland by Cahill & Co., Ltd.

CONTENTS

III ON THE INTERPRETATION OF THE TRIDENTINE DECREE ON TRADITION

PREFACE

The first chapter of this short study, contributed by Karl Rahner, is the text of a lecture delivered by him at the University of Münster in Westphalia in May 1964 on the occasion of the conferment on him of the honorary degree of Doctor of Theology. The author has left the text of his lecture unchanged, as it did not seem appropriate to him to develop it further or to provide it with a bibliography.

A rough outline of Chapter II and the text of Chapter III were delivered by Joseph Ratzinger at the meeting of the J. A. Möhler Institute (for ecumenical studies) in Paderborn on 28 March 1963. The suggestions made during the meeting, especially those by Hubert Jedin and Heinrich Schlier, encouraged the author to pursue his reflections. He subsequently rewrote his original draft of Chapter II and the revised version, reproduced here, was used by him on 28 June 1963 as an inaugural lecture on taking up the Chair of Dogmatic Theology and History of Dogma at the University of Münster. Because of the repeated call of more urgent duties the author had to abandon his original intention of expanding the two chapters. He hopes nevertheless that even in their present form his essays will contribute one or two ideas to the great debate on the theme of revelation. No attempt was, therefore, made at anything like bibliographical comprehensiveness in the notes; only the tools directly employed in the work have been mentioned there.

I

OBSERVATIONS ON THE CONCEPT OF REVELATION

by

KARL RAHNER

The correctness, the justification in a particular situation of the Church's history, and the historical import of the Church's condemnation of a heresy, do not necessarily always depend on whether the judgment passed on the heretical thesis also takes into account, and answers, the question which the fundamental tendency of that heresy raises for the Church. A positive solution of the question, which an age may in fact propound in the form of a heresy, may follow only much later. It need not be inquired whether such delay in finding a solution represents tragic guilt, error, incapacity, or is simply the tribute which the Church itself has to pay to its own historical nature. At any rate it would not be right to assume that a condemnation by the Church always falls solely on opinions and tendencies which contain nothing but an empty, dead negation of a truth long since clearly grasped and plainly proclaimed by the Church.

A half-century and more ago the heresy of Modernism threatened the Church. Among its fundamental theses and errors was its concept of revelation. For Modernism, at least if we are to judge by the systematic summary presented in the Church's condemnations, revelation was another word for the inevitable development, immanent in human history, of man's religious needs, in the course of which these needs find objective expression in the manifold forms taken by the history of religion, and slowly grow to greater purity and comprehensiveness, until they attain their objective correlate in Christianity and the Church. Such a concept was formed in antithesis to what was taken to be a view of revelation traditional in the Church, according to which revelation is the occurrence of an intervention of God "purely from outside", speaking to men and conveying to them, through the prophets, truths in human statements which they could not attain by themselves and giving commands which they must follow. The necessity of interior divine grace for the salutary acceptance by faith of that revelation was, of course, affirmed and expressly taught by the ecclesiastical orthodoxy opposed to Modernism. But the intrinsic connection between the grace of faith and historical revelation was not seen. The Church accused Modernism of immanentism, but today we are surely in a position to recognize in the average theology of that time, which is what Modernism opposed, an extrinsicism in the concept of revelation which was not the official doctrine, but was tacitly assumed by average theology. Quietly and almost unnoticed, an answer is being given at the present time to the question of a correct and full understanding of the concept of revelation, the question to which the Church at that time presumably had no clear answer and to which Modernism gave a false or overhastily decided and heretical answer. It is obvious that the question, and an adequate answer to it, are still of fundamental importance in the present confrontation and involvement of Christianity with modern intellectual life, even if the topic does not emerge very clearly and explicitly. To those who hold the anticlerical humanism of the present day, or a troubled atheism, or who think that God is an eternally indecipherable cipher, or maintain a materialism for which the hoped-for future of the mind is the real force that drives the world, it is not really the *Deus absconditus* of Christianity, dwelling in inaccessible light, that is the stumbling-block and scandal, but the doctrine that there is a *history* of revelation in which God himself prepared a single path beside the many others in the history of religion, and then himself appeared in the flesh and followed that path. The scandal is, if the expression be permitted, the categorical history of revelation within the empirical world, not the transcendental relation to God by which man has his ground in the abyss of inexpressible mystery.

What is revelation, and why, despite its immediate divine origin, is it the innermost core of human history as such? How can it be identical with the universal history of mankind, without ceasing to be the unique, special grace of God? How can revelation be present always and everywhere so that salvation can be present always and everywhere, without its ceasing on that account to be here and now, in the flesh of Christ, in the words of the prophet actually speaking in a particular place, in the letter of scripture? Can it be the innermost "motive", the real driving force of history everywhere, if it is the unique, free act of God, which cannot be calculated from below, from history, but is the miracle of his grace in a unique and irreplaceable event here and now? In order to open out the widest possible horizon for answering this question, it might be suggested that the most general relation between God and a mutable world consists in the fact that God as most immanent—and yet precisely for that reason absolutely superior to the world—confers on finite beings themselves a true active self-transcendence in their change and becoming, and is himself ultimately the future, the final cause, which represents the true and really effective cause operative in all change. Consequently it might be said that our present question is concerned with precisely the highest and most radical case of a conception which is gradually gaining ground in theology at the present time. This expresses the realization that the real coming into being of what is higher through the effective self-transcendence of an inferior cause, *and* enduring creation from above, are simply two sides, equally true and real, of the one marvel of change and history. This is seen to be the highest instance of the principle that God in his relation of freedom to his creation is, after all, not a finite cause side by side with others in the world, but is the living, permanent transcendent ground of the self-movement of the world itself. It is precisely this principle which also applies *suo modo* to the relation between God and man in the occurrence and history of revelation; in fact it applies here in the highest degree, because this history must in the highest degree be both the act of God and of man, if it is to constitute the highest reality in the being and becoming of the world. If it is possible in principle to overcome in that way the sterile antithesis of immanentism and extrinsicism in the ontological interpretation of change and history in general, then theology must also surmount such an antithesis in the question which concerns us here.

In fact if Catholic theology takes seriously its own standard doctrines of divinizing grace and God's universal salvific will, the necessity of interior elevating grace for faith, and the Thomist doctrine of the ontological, transcendental significance of entitative grace, and if theology applies those doctrines to the idea of revelation, it is quite possible, without falling into Modernism, to recognize that the history of revelation and what is usually called revelation as such, is the historical self-unfolding in predicamental terms, or, even more simply and correctly, the history of that transcendental relation between man and God which is constituted by God's self-communication, of a supernatural kind, made to every mind by grace, but inescapably and always, and which in itself can rightly be termed revelation. If transcendence always has its very being *in* history, is always mediated historically, and if man has a transcendental condition which is constituted as a permanent feature of his life as a person precisely by what we call divinizing grace by God's self-communication (not by some other causal operation), then precisely that *absolute* transcendence directed towards the absolute intimate presence of the ineffable mystery giving himself to man has a history and this is what we call the history of revelation.

The revelation event itself, therefore, always has two sides. On the one hand it constitutes man's supernaturally elevated transcendence as his permanent though grace-given destiny, always and everywhere operative, present even by the very fact of being rejected. That is the transcendental experience of the absolute and merciful closeness of God, even if it cannot be objectively expressed at will in concepts for everyone. On the other hand, the revelation event is also the historical mediation, the objective, explicit expression of the supernaturally transcendental experience. It occurs in history and, taken in its totality, constitutes the whole of history; the individual's own particular theological reflection belongs to it, though it does not constitute its primary basis or determine it. That is what is called the history of revelation in the usual sense, provided it really is the history of the true self-unfolding of the supernaturally transcendental experience and not its misinterpretation, and provided that it truly is the result of God's transcendental self-communication in grace and, therefore, occurs through God's will for such self-communication under his supernatural saving providence and is grasped as such. If this view is taken of the unity and reciprocal relationship between transcendental revelation and revelation of the predicamental and historical kind, or rather of the transcendental and historical (mediating) factors of the one revelation and its one history, a really primordial determination of what is revealed emerges: God is revealed as communicating himself in absolute, merciful presence *as* God, that is, as the absolute mystery. The historical mediation of this transcendental experience is also revealed as valid, as permitting and guaranteeing the absolute experience of God. The unique and final culmination of this history of revelation has already occurred, and in it is revealed the absolute and irrevocable unity of God's transcendental self-communication to mankind and of its historical mediation in the one God-man, who is at once God himself as communicated, the human acceptance of the communication, and the final historical manifestation of this communication and acceptance. And in this unity of God's transcendental self-communication and its final historical mediation and manifestation, the fundamental mystery of the triune God is also revealed, because what is in question is the communication of God in himself. For in that mystery it is a matter of God as he is in himself precisely inasmuch as he is God for us in history and transcendence: God in his incomprehensible primordiality, God in his real capacity to enter man's transcendence and his history, Father, Spirit and Son. Inasmuch as history mediates transcendence, the Son sends the Spirit; inasmuch as transcendence makes history, the Spirit effects the incarnation of the Logos; inasmuch as appearance in history signifies the manifestation of reality, the incarnate Logos is revealed as the self-utterance of the Father in truth; inasmuch as God's coming among us in the centre of our personal life signifies his love and ours, the Pneuma is revealed in his own proper self as Love. It is by making the experience, through the intermediary of history, of the transcendental absolute presence of God in his self-communication, and accepting it, by means of itself, that we in fact know at all, in that act of faith, what we mean when we speak of God's Trinity, and briefly express by it the form and content of our Christian faith and of its revelation and revelation history, and are baptized in those three names.

The fundamental idea of revelation which we have sketched roughly and rapidly in this way may, perhaps, be elucidated as regards its basis and consequences by a few rather random reflections.

If what has been said is correct, then transcendental and predicamental revelation and the history of revelation are co-extensive with the spiritual history of mankind as such. That is not a Modernist error but a Christian truth which can be verified very simply, for it can safely be asserted that the history of supernatural salvation is operative everywhere in history; this has been driven even more forcefully into the Church's consciousness of its faith by the pronouncements of Vatican II. But salvation without faith, and faith without genuine revelation, is impossible. It is not necessary to explain the possibility of revelation and faith outside the Old and New Testament history of revelation and faith by a special Catholic theory such as that of Straub or of Billot, or by having recourse to an explicit, empirical tradition deriving from primitive revelation, in which Adam's actual experience is supposed to have been transmitted in propositional, doctrinal form. That is scarcely probable in view of our present knowledge of the history of religion and of mankind, which may have extended over two million years. It is only necessary to assume—and the data of present-day theology support this—that every human being is elevated by grace in his transcendental intellectuality in a non-reflex manner; that this "entitative" divinization—which is proffered to freedom, even if it is not accepted freely in faith—involves a transcendental divinization of the fundamental subjective attitude, the ultimate horizon of man's knowledge and freedom, in the perspective of which he accomplishes his life. If this is so, that supernatural feature characterizing man's life as a person, absolutely every man's, constitutes in fact a revelation of God through his self-communication in grace. And that grace-given fundamental subjective attitude of man, which is directed towards the God of triune life, can quite definitely be regarded as a word-revelation, provided the notion of word is not reduced to that of a phonetic utterance and provided that it is not forgotten that such transcendental revelation is always historically mediated and that man's historical reality can never be without language. It never consists of dead facts; the interpretation of the facts is itself a constitutive factor in every historical event. No revelation in conceptual, objective terms of particular objects or propositions is given solely by the transcendentally experienced openness of man to the triune God of eternal life. But what this gives is something more, something which forms the basis of all the articles of faith and is the condition of their very possibility, what alone makes them really the words of God: the supernatural horizon of experience of an *a priori* kind, the light of faith as such, as we could quite simply say in the traditional way, provided that we are still able to take seriously and understand such well-worn words of tradition. Let us insist once again that it is not, of course, meant by all this that the transcendental *a priori* openness of man to the God of eternal life and of absolute self-communication can be non-historical, isolated, pursuing some mystical existence or other of its own in individualistic introspection outside history. It is necessarily accomplished in the history of the action and thought of mankind, and may be so in a very explicit or in a quite anonymous way. Consequently there is never a history of transcendental revelation in isolation. History in the concrete, both individually and collectively, is the history of God's transcendental revelation. Of course, such concrete history is never revelation history pure and simple. The latter takes place in the former, always in an indissoluble unity with error, misinterpretation, guilt, abuses; it is a history both just and sinful, all the more so as we really must say *simul iustus et peccator* here where the history of sin and that of salvation inextricably mingle until God's judgment comes. That in no way excludes the possibility of a genuine history of revelation in the whole history of humanity, as can be seen, for example, from the fact that for Christians it is only possible to discern and distinguish, in the religious history of the Old Testament, between the genuine history of revelation and a sinful, proud religious history on the basis of Christ and never merely by standards provided by the Old Testament itself. Only in Christ do even the holy scriptures of the Old Testament possess an inner and external canon as a guiding principle of their own interpretation; yet they have to be recognized by the Christian as a genuine history of the revelation of the Father of our Lord.[1]

Even those who want to work out the idea of revelation entirely on the basis of encounter with the word of God, preached or written, finally meet with the transcendental side of the revelation event. For they require a canon within a canon; to them the spoken and written word only becomes the word of God absolutely as such in the interior grace-given occurrence of faith, and the external message of faith is demythologized into a transcendental form. If religious history is that part of human history generally in which the theological nature of man is not only accomplished in fact (as in all history), but also becomes the focus of explicit attention, then the history of religion is at the same time the most explicit part of the history of revelation and the intellectual region in which historical misinterpretations of the transcendental experience of God occur most plainly and with the most serious consequences, and where superstition most clearly flourishes. But it is always a case of both and always an ambiguity which for us is inextricable.

In the Catholic scholastic theology of the last centuries, in contrast to that of the Middle Ages, preferential treatment has been given to the question of the testimony paid to the messenger of revelation by miracles performed in the presence of hearers summoned to believe, but the question of the revelation-occurrence in the bearer of revelation, the prophet himself, has not been dealt with or has been dealt with inadequately. From what has been said, it would follow that the theology of the process of the act of faith and that of the revelation-occurrence are to a large extent identical. Catholic fundamental theology is, therefore, entirely right from the point of view of method when it deals, as at least it often does, with the so-called *analysis fidei,* when rightly understood, within its own sphere. At all events that would be the correct procedure, provided it were used to study the point where faith and the reception of revelation can still be seen in their original unity. There the transcendental side of the original reception of revelation and that of faith coincide: man is constituted through grace as affected by God's ontological self-communication and in radical freedom accepts this constitutive feature of his human reality.

For Catholic theology, the question of demythologization is still largely concentrated in the concrete problem of whether what fundamental theology calls miracles are possible, what their significance is and whether they can be recognized. On the basis of the fundamental idea which we have just outlined it might be explicitly inquired whether in this whole matter we should not really lend greater weight to the view that the mediation of a transcendental experience of God cannot itself adequately be mediated once again, but that it always implies the trusting awareness of the prior presence of the unmediated. Consequently it is impossible in principle to distinguish adequately and explicitly between mediation through the bare fact of so-called objective reality and mediation through the interpretative representation of that bare fact. Nor is it necessary, because the mediation has its ultimate truth in what is mediated. For that reason someone who, with the intention of demythologizing, distinguishes them purely and simply, and someone who posits both the mediation and what is mediated as equally absolute, both miss in the same way the ontological difference and unity between what is predicamental and what is transcendental, as well as the difference yet indestructible unity between the mediation of so-called historical fact and its interpretation. It must then, of course, also be remembered that this mediation, being an historical one, is necessarily always social; it is "ecclesial" in the deepest sense of the word. It, therefore, includes an acceptance of the never totally analysed or explicitly self-conscious belief of the Church, the community of believers. That belief of the Church is always, whether in the Church or in the individual, a unity of sign and truth beyond man's disposal or decision. And as in the word of the sacrament and in the Word incarnate, sign and truth are given inseparably and unmixed, and are not merely brought together by the faith of the believer.

On that basis it might become clear just what *fides implicita* is, which nowadays, unfortunately, plays a smaller part even in Catholic theology than it should. Fundamentally it means that all categorically explicit faith, as such, lays hold of a sign and is, therefore, truly faith only if it grasps the sign through being itself held in the grasp of the unutterable mystery of the presence of God mercifully communicating himself, and only if it is always aware that the finite mediation has the character of a sign, and one that belongs to the Church and is found in the Church. And since the holy darkness of the incomprehensible God is not abolished, but rather, on the contrary, definitely established by revelation and is accepted as it is with adoration and love, the "implicit" character of what is really revealed in the word of revelation, and the character of one's own faith as "implicit" in that of the Church, both belong to the very nature of revelation and faith and are not factors which are only present when the *rudes* and the ignorant hear revelation and believe.

This throws light on a well-known phenomenon of the history of religion and of Christian dogma: the continually renewed attempt to reduce the totality of the many-sided and extensive dogmatic theology and institutions of a religion to a kernel, to what alone is truly important, however this single decisive element is named and discovered. On this point it can now be said, on the basis of the unity of transcendental and predicamental revelation which we have indicated, that such a single essential element in religion does exist, but is not replaced by any reduction which remains within the framework of the categories, nor is it thereby experienced more directly or with more certainty. Moreover, if Christianity is to be the absolute religion of all and is not to represent a particular covenant of a particular people with God, it cannot cease to confess Christ as the mediator and bringer of salvation in such a way that he integrates in himself, in his truly corporeal nature present in this world, every conceivable mediation by all that is real, so that he relativizes and at the same time definitively posits this. There is, therefore, no point at which, in this mediation of his, other things have to be excluded entirely and on principle, whether they be word, liturgical sign, the Church's social reality, the ministry, imagery, or even secular things. Yet despite the plurality of the mediation, and despite the legitimacy of all its aspects and the obligatory character that *per se* belongs to it, the possibility nevertheless remains that, in the various times and places which the one God of grace has determined even under the new covenant, the urgency and perceptibility of various particular mediations may, even when they are enduringly valid, themselves possess a history. Such a history of the definitive revelation in Christ, within the final and eternal aeon, may still be mirrored even now, in its legitimacy as willed by God, in the tragical history of divided Christendom, whose divisions reflect the genuine multiplicity of the many mediations of the one revelation, and while they accuse us, nevertheless promise us the grace of God.

On the basis of the unity and distinction between transcendental revelation and predicamental, historical revelation, which imply that the same distinction and the same unity are also found in faith, an indication can be discerned that the subjective disposition of the believer must be thought of as distinct from faith and yet as one with it. If we leave out of account for a moment the very incidental mention of grace

22

which is all that is commonly found in theological descriptions of faith, the character of faith as coming by hearing is explained in such an empirical and *a posteriori* manner in relation to certain defined articles of faith that the word of faith appears to be addressed to hearing almost as if it were a quite unexceptional formal capacity to grasp any true proposition once it is understood, and provided it is presented correctly with its proper grounds in an appropriate way. The *a priori* capacity to believe is itself scarcely taken into consideration in Catholic theology, the subjective disposition, that is to say. As an *a priori* capacity for revelation and faith, this must not, of course, be thought of as a localized faculty side by side with others, as a sort of particular sentiment, an intrinsically limited "need" or something of the sort. It would have to be understood as the union of what we have called the transcendental aspect of revelation with the *a priori* capacity (identical with the whole transcendental character of man), for God's self-communication in grace; for it is by these two that God's transcendental revelation is constituted. Moreover, both of these would have to be understood, not in a merely factual objective sense, but in an ontological, subjective sense.

Every Catholic analysis of faith declares the "authority of God" to be the highest, ultimate and sole "formal object" and "motive" of faith. As often as not, inextricable difficulties then arise, because this "authority" is itself thought of as mediated empirically by *a posteriori* cognition, and so determined by the horizon of human knowledge. Yet it must go beyond such an horizon if the word is to remain really the word of God and is not to be reduced by the *a priori* conditions of human cognition to the purely created level. But if when

23

revelation and faith occur, God himself in his own self-communication is what is believed and is the *a priori* principle of belief, and if the logic of faith is not a predicamental logic learnt from without, but, like the natural logic which is spontaneously exercised, is the intrinsic ontological structure of the act of faith itself, and if the external message of faith does not supply the *a posteriori* motive of faith, but brings the *a priori* motive directly into relation with itself, then the problem in question disappears. In that way it also becomes more understandable why a materially false act of faith can be a genuine act of faith and not just a human act of recognition of a formal object grasped *a posteriori* under merely human mental conditions.

Of necessity we interrupt these suggestions. In all that has been said, we have only been able to give some pointers to the direction in which a solution may be found to a problem which has seemed topical since the days of Modernism and which nonetheless appears in some way to have been evaded. Even by such a slight example, but one which may be regarded as typical of many other unsolved theological problems, it can be seen how laboriously and slowly theological work advances. Patience and forbearance are required—and the conviction that while theology does not produce the Christian's faith, it is nevertheless called upon really and truly to serve it, and to serve it today.

In expressing my respectful and cordial thanks to the Theological Faculty of the University of Münster for the great honour it has conferred on me, I do so in the consciousness that those who are engaged in the task of building up the structure of theology labour in vain unless the Lord builds too, that we must work while it is still day, that all *theologia mentis* cannot be more than an assistance to the *theologia cordis et vitae,* and that all theology is in fact simply an attempt to build a way which loses itself in the mystery of God, where there is no way, but who nevertheless lets himself be found.

II

REVELATION AND TRADITION

by

JOSEPH RATZINGER

1. *Statement of the problem*

The question of the way in which the word of revelation uttered in Christ remains present in history and reaches men is one of the fundamental questions which split western Christendom in the age of the Reformation. The conflict concerned the idea of "tradition" in which Catholic Christendom sought to express a form of transmission of revelation additional to that of holy scripture. This provoked a double protest. By tradition, in the first place the so-called *consuetudines ecclesiae* were meant, for example Sunday observance, turning to the east for prayer, customs connected with fasting, various consecrations and blessings and other things of that kind which gave the Church's piety in the later Middle Ages its particular stamp. The innumerable things, some edifying, others surprising, which made the late mediaeval Church a rambling, complicated house, full of nooks and corners, were justified by the idea of "tradition" and declared to be a legitimate, integral part of concrete Christian reality.[1] But in the light of his experience of God's judgment and mercy, Luther, struck by the simplicity of the gospel and its explosive force, could see nothing but frivolity in all those "traditions" by which men, he thought, were deceived about the real abyss of their nature and superficially pacified. He even saw in these things the return of the Law, the precedence given to human enactments over God's word, against which Paul had fought so inexorably and which nevertheless had now become a reality in the Church again. The Confession of Augsburg also deals with this matter. It lists a series of precepts which, according to current doctrine, could involve mortal sin: the prohibition of manual labour on Sundays and holy days, the obligation of saying Office, the laws of fasting etc. It then goes on, "Where do the bishops derive the right and power to impose such burdens on Christendom to ensnare consciences? For St Peter in the Acts of the Apostles, chapter 15, forbade a yoke to be put on the necks of the disciples. And St Paul tells the Corinthians that authority was given to them to improve, not to harm. Why then do they increase sin by such impositions? . . . If the bishops have power to burden the Churches with innumerable impositions and ensnare consciences, why does divine scripture so often forbid us to make or to listen to human precepts? Why does it call them 'devil's doctrines'? Has the Holy Spirit warned against all such things in vain?"[2] The theme of *traditio* is here transformed into that of *abusus*. Tradition is a human invention by which man hides himself from God or, rather, rebels against him in order to take his salvation into his own hands instead of hoping for it from the favour of the Lord which cannot be claimed or extorted. To tradition, understood as an enactment, is opposed the message of grace. "For the great article of the gospel must always be maintained that we obtain the grace of God through faith in Christ without merit on our part and do not merit it by a service of God, instituted by men." [3]

The problem of tradition, however, also became acute from another point of view which in turn did not lead to any more positive a solution. When Luther discovered the gospel within the gospel, he had at the same time the impression that he had liberated the word of God from the fetters imposed by the Church's ministry, which had possessed itself of this word and no longer allowed it to make its own valid statement, but employed it arbitrarily. This idea that the word of God is fettered in the Catholic Church through its connection with the authority of the ministry is repeatedly expressed in the writings of the Reformers. The most moving example perhaps, humanly speaking, is that of Melanchthon. He was willing to compromise, and when he signed Luther's Smalkaldic Articles, it was with the proviso: ". . . as regards the pope, however, I think that if he were willing to allow the gospel, for the sake of peace and common unity . . . we should allow (and concede) his superiority over the bishops which he possesses *iure humano*".[4] The idea also influenced the conception expressed in the Confession of Augsburg when it speaks of the Church as the *congregatio sanctorum, in qua evangelium pure docetur et recte administrantur sacramenta.*[5] The Church is, therefore, essentially determined by two things, pure doctrine and sacraments rightly administered. There is no mention of the ministry. In fact, this silence is no less important for the notion of the Church in the Confession of Augsburg than what is actually said, for it is quite clearly deliberate and represents the exact antithesis to what was then, and still is, the valid Catholic conception of the Church as defined by three elements : *fides* (corresponding to *pure docere*) —*communio* (corresponding to *sacramenta*)—*auctoritas*.[6] Ministry here appears as the criterion of the word. It guarantees the word. With Melanchthon it is the other way round; for him the word is the criterion of the ministry, which ultimately is tested by the yard-stick of the word, and, measured by it, may become liable to rejection. The word has become independent; it stands on its own as a reality superior to the ministry. Perhaps in this reversal of the relations between word and ministry lies the real opposition between the views of the Church held by Catholics and Reformers. At the same time it coincided with the contrast in their views of tradition. For rejection of the ministry as the criterion of the word logically meant the reduction of the word to scripture as its own interpreter, and scripture now remained as the only authentic form of the word and tolerated no independent reality, "tradition", beside it.

The Council of Trent in its struggle for the concept of tradition had these two bases of the Reformers' criticism in mind and endeavoured to formulate an answer to them. It is striking to observe how, in view of the Lutheran equation of *traditio* and *abusus*, the themes of *traditio* and *reformatio* become interwoven for the Council, and how the Fathers again and again were confronted with the dilemma whether to answer Luther's attack on tradition first with a definition of tradition or to begin with *reformatio*, removing abuses.[7] As

29

regards doctrine, Trent of course rejected both the Reformation reproaches. Trent continued to maintain that the word is not a reality standing independently above the Church, but that it is delivered by the Lord to the Church. Nor is it thereby exposed to random caprice but precisely in that way remains in his own hands out of reach of human arbitrariness. In the view of the Fathers of Trent it probably seemed fundamentally a form of weakness in faith to be anxious for the word committed to the Church as though the Church might, as it were, outgrow it in such a way that recourse would have to be had to the word against the Church; they were indubitably certain that the Lord who instituted the Church as his Body is also able to preserve it for his word.

Today, 400 years later, it must be admitted that in the opposition that divided Luther and Trent, the dilemma of western Christendom is still manifest, by the way it appears once again, for example, in the correspondence between Harnack and Peterson. Peterson pointed out, when expressing thanks for Harnack's article "The Old Testament in the Pauline Epistles and the Pauline Churches", that Harnack, in the way he had dealt with the relation between scripture and its interpretation, had expressed not the Protestant, but the Catholic principle. Harnack replied, " It is a truism that the so-called 'formal principle' of earlier Protestantism is a critical impossibility, and compared with it the Catholic principle is *formally* the better; but materially the Catholic principle of tradition damages history much more (both as rank growth and under the shears of the magisterium), because fortunately the New Testament actually comprises the best sources".[8] In this rather slovenly formulation with its opposition of formal and material aspects, the old dilemma once more appears. Can the word be given over to the Church without fear that it will forfeit its own power and vitality under the shears of the magisterium or in the rank growth of the *sensus fidelium*? That is the Protestant's question to the Catholic. Can the word be posited as independent without thereby delivering it up to the caprice of exegetes, evacuating it of meaning in the controversies of historians and so robbing it entirely of binding force? That is the counter-question which the Catholic will immediately put, and he will also be of the opinion that in any case we have not to consider whether we are going to commit the word to the Church or not. The Catholic will say that the Lord himself *has* delivered it to the Church. It is true that this will not prevent him, if he honestly looks the facts in the face, from regarding concern for the purity of the word as a duty of the greatest gravity, which is not fulfilled simply by appealing to the infallibility of the Church. To that extent Luther's struggle for the word will seriously appear to him as at least a salutary warning.

In the 400 years since the Reformation, however, history has not stood still, even in theology. Two tendencies can be observed in regard to the relation between the denominations and their theology. On the one hand, after the rupture each dug itself in and consolidated its own position, and each group from then on had its own history and continued to develop on its own, far from the other. On the other hand, the distance so created permitted greater objectivity in regard to the other and so in the end, in spite of everything, there is an increasing tendency for each to break out of its own special history and to make contact again with the other. Probably the most achieve a new view of the problem of tradition while over-coming one-sided anti-Reformation positions has been made by important attempt in our generation on the Catholic side to the Tübingen dogmatic theologian J. R. Geiselmann. His endeavours exercised a valuable influence even on the dis-cussions of the Second Vatican Council and gave the Council's wrestling with this question that exciting topicality which raised it, in the very first session, from a doctrinal dispute between different schools of theologians to a serious reflection by Catholic Christendom on its own essential foundations.[9] Geiselmann's thesis is well-known and only needs to be out-lined briefly here in order to provide the starting-point for a consideration of the question in an endeavour to dig deeper and perhaps advance the discussion a little.

Geiselmann's starting-point is a new interpretation of the pronouncements of the Council of Trent on the nature of tradition. Trent had laid down that the truth of the gospel is contained *in libris scriptis et sine scripto traditionibus*. That was and still is interpreted as meaning that scripture does not contain the whole truth of the gospel, and that consequently no *sola scriptura* is possible because part of the truth of revela-tion is conveyed to us solely through tradition. Geiselmann took up the point that had already been indicated by others, that the first draft of the text had been worded so that truth is contained *partim in libris scriptis partim in sine scripto traditionibus*. In that way, therefore, the doctrine of the division of revealed truth between two sources (scripture and tradition) would have been clearly expressed. But the Council abandoned the *partim-partim* and was satisfied with the simple link *et*. Geiselmann concludes from this that the Council had turned away from the idea of a division of revealed truth between two separate sources or at least had not expressly defined it. And he draws the further conclusion that even as a Catholic theologian one can hold the view of the material sufficiency of scripture. In other words, even a Catholic can maintain that holy scripture adequately transmits revelation to us. Consequently Geiselmann regards a material *sola scriptura* principle as quite acceptable for a Catholic and even thinks he can show that it has a much stronger tradition in its favour and that the Council of Trent itself meant to point in this direction.[10]

It is easy to understand that such a thesis could reckon on a good deal of agreement in various quarters in view of the quite new possibilities of contact between Catholics and Protestants which it seemed to open out.[11] It seems to me quite indisputable that it represents in fact a considerable material advance. Yet as soon as the thesis is rather more closely examined in regard to its historical and intrinsic grounds, a whole series of difficulties emerge that make it impossible to rest content with it. In the second part of this essay we shall attempt a few remarks on the historical side of the problem. For the moment we shall turn directly to the actual problems themselves which immediately prompt the question, what exactly does " sufficiency of scripture " mean? Geiselmann himself, as a Catholic theologian, has to hold fast to Catholic dogmas as such, but none of them is to be had *sola scriptura*, neither the great dogmas of Christian antiquity, of what was once the *consensus quinquesaecularis,* nor, even less, the new ones of 1854 and 1950. In that case, however, what sense is there in talking about the sufficiency of scripture? Does it not threaten to become a dangerous delusion with which we deceive first ourselves and then others (or perhaps do not in fact do anything of the kind)? At least, in order to maintain both that scripture contains all revealed truth and that the dogma of 1950, for example, is a revealed truth, recourse has to be had to such a wide sense of the term "sufficiency" that the word loses all serious meaning.

In this way, however, the second and really decisive question arises. Does concern for the idea of the sufficiency of scripture really come to grips at all with the real problem of the notion of tradition, or is it a case of lingering over a relatively superficial symptom of a state of affairs that lies much deeper? The introductory remarks from which we started should have made it clear that the answer must plainly be "yes". The question of the sufficiency of scripture is a purely secondary problem within the framework of a much more fundamental decision which confronted us earlier in the terms *abusus* and *auctoritas* and which, therefore, concerns the relation between the authority of the Church and the authority of holy scripture. Everything else depends on the way this is understood. In order to advance, it will therefore be necessary to penetrate deeper and not to linger over such immediately visible but secondary matters as the sufficiency or insufficiency of scripture. The comprehensive problem of the mode of presence of the revealed word among the faithful must be dealt with as a whole. Then it becomes clear that we must go behind the positive sources, scripture and tradition, to their inner source, revelation, the living word of God from which scripture and tradition spring and without which their significance for faith cannot be understood. The question of "scripture and tradition" remains insoluble as long as it is not expanded into a question of "revelation and tradition" and thus inserted into the larger context to which it belongs. Consequently in what follows, I should like to attempt to develop positively in thesis form, without going into details of possible discussions, the concept of tradition in relation to its intrinsic function, in the hope of giving at least a partial answer to the Reformers' question, so that the whole essay might prove to be a moment in a dialogue, the necessity of which is being recognized more and more clearly by all.

2. Theses on the relation between revelation and tradition

a) Revelation and scripture

A first thesis on this set of problems might be formulated as follows, bearing in mind the patristic conception of scripture and revelation. The fact that "tradition" exists is primarily based on the non-identity of the two realities, "revelation" and "scripture". Revelation means God's whole speech and action with man; it signifies a *reality* which scripture makes known but which is not itself simply identical with scripture. Revelation, therefore, is more than scripture to the extent that reality exceeds information about it.[12] It might also be said that scripture is the material principle of revelation (perhaps the only one, perhaps one side by side with others—a question that can be left open for the moment), but that it is not revelation itself. That is something of which the Reformers were still perfectly well aware; it was only in the subsequent controversy between post-Tridentine Catholic theology and Protestant orthodoxy that it was noticeably obscured.[13] In the present century it has been Protestant theologians such as Barth and Brunner who have rediscovered this fact which was taken absolutely as a matter of course both by patristic and by mediaeval theology.[14]

What we have said can be made clear from another angle. There can be scripture without revelation. For revelation always and only becomes a reality where there is faith. The unbeliever remains under the veil of which Paul speaks in 2 Corinthians 3.[15] He can read scripture and know what it contains. He can even understand, purely conceptually, what is meant and how its statements cohere, yet he has no share in the revelation. Revelation is in fact fully present only when, in addition to the material statements which testify to it, its own inner reality is itself operative in the form of faith. Consequently revelation to some degree includes its recipient, without whom it does not exist. Revelation cannot be pocketed like a book one carries around. It is a living reality which calls for the living man as the location of its presence.

In view of what has been said, we may, therefore, affirm that revelation goes beyond the fact of scripture in two respects: as a reality deriving from God it always extends upwards into God's action; as a reality which makes itself known to man in faith, it also extends beyond the fact of scripture which serves to mediate it.

This non-coincidence of scripture and revelation makes it clear that quite apart from the question whether scripture is the sole material source or not, there can never really, properly speaking, be a *sola scriptura* in regard to Christianity. As we have already said, that was still clear in principle to the great Reformers, and only fell into oblivion in what has been called Protestant orthodoxy. Scripture *is* not revelation but at most only a part of the latter's greater reality.

b) The different significance of scripture in the old and new covenants

The specifically Christian problems of revelation, scripture and tradition are further determined by the double form of revelation in the old and new covenants, to which the double form of scripture in the Old and New Testaments corresponds. Just as the two covenants are different in kind, so too is the fact of scripture not identical in the two cases. That is very plain in the New Testament writings, which understand by "scripture" only the Old Testament. This for them is and remains "scripture", the meaning of which has, they are convinced, come to light in the Christ-event.[16] Consequently they do not oppose to the old scripture, or set side by side with it, a new scripture, but they place in contrast to the one single scripture, i.e. the Old Testament, the Christ-event as the spirit which explains scripture, a fundamental conception which also determined the form of the oldest creeds and alone renders them intelligible. The formula "Jesus is the Christ" in fact signifies that in the historical Jesus the Christ-message of the Old Testament is fulfilled, that who Jesus is, can be understood on the basis of the Old Testament and the meaning of the Old Testament perceived in the light of the Christ-event. This conception appears very distinctly in Paul, for on its basis he even contrasts the old and new covenants as *gramma* and *pneuma,* i.e. as letter (scripture) and spirit (2 Cor 3:6-18), and designates the Lord as the *pneuma* who makes scripture intelligible, or is its meaning, its true, living (not merely literary) content (2 Cor 3:14-18). Paul probably draws on the idea of the new covenant as Jeremiah expresses it (31:33f): no scripture is needed any more, for the Law is written in the heart, and no further external instruction is required, because God himself teaches men. John expresses the same thought, with reference to Deutero-Isaiah (54:13), when he describes the era that began with Christ as the time in which all are taught by God himself. And Peter's Pentecostal discourse, handed down to us by Acts (2:14-36), develops the same idea with reference to Joel (3:1-5). In each case the time inaugurated by the Christ-event appears as the answer to a line of hope, which expected that in the future age scripture would, in an ultimate sense, be rendered actually superfluous by the immediate proximity of the divine teacher in man himself. If the foregoing testimonies to this thought are examined, it will be seen that the restriction of the term "scripture" to the writings of the old covenant is not merely a momentary question of terminology, due to the lack of actual New Testament writings, and one which lost all significance in the second half of the second century with the gradual formation of the New Testament canon. A conviction is expressed there, the meaning of which is of course more difficult to recognize since the actual New Testament scripture arose, but which is not thereby replaced or cancelled.

One thing is, therefore, clear. In the new order of salvation which began with Christ, "scripture" occupies a different position from the one it had under the old covenant. Consequently it is not necessary to consider to what extent the old covenant's own conception of its own nature is rightly represented. It certainly was not from the start the covenant of the *gramma*, of scripture held to be self-sufficient in the way in which it appears in St Paul's description.[17] And from Jeremiah and Deutero-Isaiah onwards there appears a longing to go beyond the *gramma* in a new immediacy of the Spirit of God, probably simultaneous with an ever more intense development of a scriptural principle which caused scripture more and more to become the Law which does not make man live, but kills. However that may be, in the New Testament view the Old Testament appears as "scripture" in the proper sense, which reached its true meaning through the Christ-event, by being drawn into the living sphere of the Christ-reality. And if scripture has also come into existence *de facto* in the New Testament, scripture can no longer have that conclusive and exclusive sense which belonged to it, according to the Pauline conception, in the Old Testament, but is rather the means of opening out the Old Testament into the wide vistas of the Christ-event. It is, as it were, the arrested process of the new exposition of scripture with Christ as basis. At all events it has no desire to be independent, to be shut in on itself in literal exposition of a text, but can only subsist within the spiritual reality of Jesus Christ, who remains with his own "always, to the close of the age" (Mt 28:20), who by his going through the Cross has come again in the Holy Spirit (as John expresses it) and, through the Spirit, expounds to the disciples what they once were still unable to bear, when the Lord still visibly dwelt among them (Jn 16:12 f.).

c) Christ the revelation of God

The actual reality which occurs in Christian revelation is nothing and no other than Christ himself. He is revelation in the proper sense: "He who has seen me, has seen the Father", Christ says in John (14:9). This means that the reception of revelation is equivalent to entering into the Christ-reality, the source of that double state of affairs which Paul alternately describes with the words "Christ in us" and "we in Christ".

In this process, the reception of individual propositions is secondary; they are only meaningful at all as ways of rendering explicit the one mystery of Christ. That very fact throws light on the question of the material sufficiency of scripture which, since Geiselmann's writings, has so dominated the discussion. The question has to be raised, after all, what from a Christian point of view, material sufficiency can mean. It is only the Christ-*reality* which is "sufficient". Materially speaking, its content can be stated with greater or less explicitness, but that is ultimately not decisive, and for that reason it is quite possible for that content to be given further explicit formulation *subsequent* to scripture. This will have to be dealt with more closely in a moment.

The same state of affairs can also be regarded from another angle, which permits an advance. The reception of revelation, in which the Christ-reality becomes ours, is called in biblical language "faith". From this point of view perhaps it is clearer why, for the New Testament, faith is equivalent to the indwelling of Christ. If we firmly hold that for scripture the presence of revelation is equivalent to the presence of Christ, a further step follows. We find the presence of Christ designated in two further ways. It appears on the one hand, as we have already seen, identical with the faith (Eph 3:17), in which the individual encounters Christ and in him enters the sphere of influence of his saving power. But it is also hidden under the Pauline term of "Body of Christ" which of course implies that the community of the faithful, the Church, represents Christ's continued abiding in this world in order to gather men into, and make them share, his mighty presence.[18]

These two aspects taken together mean, therefore, that faith is entry into Christ's presence, into the abiding reality of Christ to which scripture bears witness but with which scripture itself is not simply and solely identical. It also follows that the presence of revelation is essentially connected with the two realities "faith" and "Church", which themselves, as is now clear, are closely connected. This in turn leads back to what was stated in the first thesis, that revelation goes beyond scripture in two respects, in relation to God and in relation to its human recipient. That statement, which at first was rather indefinite, is now found to possess an essentially concrete meaning in relation to actual Christian realities.

d) The nature of tradition

The explicitation of the Christ-reality, which is revelation and which has its double yet single enduring presence in faith and in the Church, occurs in the proclamation of the gospel. This preaching, therefore, by its very nature is an unfolding, a making explicit, and it is so in two ways, corresponding to the double form of revelation in the old covenant and the new. It is an interpretation of the Old Testament on the basis of the

Christ-event and as orientated towards that event. It is also an interpretation of the Christ-event itself on the basis of the *pneuma,* which means on the basis of the Church's present. The latter is possible because Christ is not dead but living, not only Christ yesterday but Christ today and tomorrow. But it is precisely in his Church that he is living and present; in the Church which is his Body in which his Spirit is active. Light still needs to be thrown on this from the nature of the Church. As the New Testament shows, Jesus's message was at first a directly eschatological one, directed towards the kingdom of God, not towards the Church. The existence of a Church is not, of course, in contradiction to that message, but in the perspective of the message it is nevertheless only secondary. Similarly the activity of the Twelve after Pentecost was not in the first place directed to the Church but to the kingdom of God. It is one of the striking facts that can clearly be observed from the Acts of the Apostles that the Twelve at first did not undertake a mission to the gentile nations but endeavoured to convert Israel and so to realize the necessary conditions for the kingdom. It was only the shock of various historical events, especially the execution of Stephen, that of James and, decisively, the arrest and flight of Peter, which brought the original community, as the sources show, to recognize the failure of the attempt to convert Israel as definitive, and consequently to go to the pagans and so create the Church instead of the kingdom. They did this, as the reports, particularly the 15th chapter of Acts, show, as a new decision in the Holy Spirit. By doing so they opened out that new interpretation of the message of Christ which is the essential basis of the Church.[19]

This proceeding, whereby the definitive establishment of the Church rests on a decision "in the Holy Spirit", is the reason why there is the Church's interpretation of the New Testament just as there is a Christological interpretation of the Old Testament and why we must consequently note the following facts which are to be distinguished even though they are interconnected in the *analogia fidei*.

(i) There is an Old Testament theology of the Old Testament which the historian draws out from the Old Testament itself. It already unfolds there in a series of superimposed strata, in which old texts are read anew in the light of new events and receive new interpretations. The phenomenon of further growth of texts in new situations, of the further growth of revelation by new interpretations of the old, already determines in a quite essential way the internal structure of the Old Testament itself.[20]

(ii) There is a New Testament theology of the Old Testament which is not identical with the actual intrinsic Old Testament theology of the Old Testament, though it is linked to it in the unity of the *analogia fidei*.[21] Perhaps on this basis it is even possible to say in a new way what the *analogia fidei* between the two testaments means. The New Testament theology of the Old Testament is, as we have said, not identical with the actual intrinsic and historically observable Old Testament theology of the Old Testament; it is a new interpretation in the light of the Christ-event which does not arise from the purely historical consideration of the Old Testament alone. By carrying out such a re-interpretation, it nevertheless does not do something which is completely alien to the nature of the Old Testament, approaching it merely from the outside, but continues the inner structural pattern of the Old Testament, which itself lived and grew by such re-interpretations. (iii) There is a New Testament theology of the New Testament, corresponding to the Old Testament theology of the Old Testament; in other words, the theology which the historian as such can derive from the New Testament itself. It too is characterized and given its structure by a similar growth, by a similar new understanding of the old in a new situation.

(iv) There is a Church theology of the New Testament which we call dogmatic theology. It is related to the New Testament theology of the New Testament in the same way that the New Testament theology of the Old Testament is related to the Old Testament theology of the Old Testament. What is actually "additional", and what, therefore, distinguishes dogmatic theology from biblical theology, is what we call, in a precise sense, tradition. Here, too, it would have to be emphasized once again that the Church's theology of the New Testament, although not simply identical with the intrinsic and historically observable New Testament theology of the New Testament, but going beyond it, is nevertheless not purely extrinsic to it. For here too, in the actual New Testament itself, there begins the process of the Church's interpretation of what is handed down; the Church's theology of the New Testament extends as a process into the heart of the New Testament itself, as could perhaps be most clearly shown by the history of the synoptic tradition.[22]

Another remark must be made. Though we have just equated the Church's theology of the New Testament with dogmatic theology, closer inspection will show that a further distinction is necessary. For dogmatic theology as a branch of scientific study includes, of course, in addition to the Church's interpretation of the New Testament, the private theology of individual theologians. Consequently, in a precise sense we could designate only dogma as such as the Church's theology of the New Testament. In any case the scheme indicated only represents, of course, a general outline which would need clarification and distinctions before it could be considered exact. For our purpose, however, this rough sketch may suffice. Summarizing what has been said, we can now observe several sources of the reality called "tradition" and, consequently, several strata within it.

First source: The extent to which the reality of "revelation" is more than "scripture".

Second source: The specific character of New Testament revelation as *pneuma*, as opposed to *gramma*, and consequently what one might call in Bultmann's terminology, the impossibility of objectivizing it. This state of affairs has been expressed in the Church's practice and, as a consequence, in mediaeval theology, by the placing of *fides* above *scriptura,* that is to say, of the creed as rule of faith above the details of what is written.[23] The creed appears as the hermeneutical key to scripture which without interpretation must ultimately remain dumb.

Third source: The character of the Christ-event as present and the authoritative enduring presence of Christ's Spirit in his Body the Church and, connected with this, the authority to interpret Christ yesterday in relation to Christ today, the origin of which we have observed in the Church's reinterpretation by the apostles of the message of the kingdom.

Corresponding to these three sources of the concept of tradition (or, better, of the reality which we term tradition), the following strata in tradition can perhaps be discerned.

(i) At the beginning of all tradition stands the fact that the Father gives the Son over to the world and that the Son for his part allows himself to be given over to the "nations", as a sign. This original *paradosis,* in its character as judgment and gift of salvation, is continued in the abiding presence of Christ in his Body, the Church. To that extent the whole mystery of Christ's continuing presence is primarily the whole reality which is transmitted in tradition, the decisive fundamental reality which is antecedent to all particular explicit expressions of it, even those of scripture, and which represents what has in fact to be handed down.

(ii) Tradition then exists concretely as presence in faith, which again, as the in-dwelling of Christ, is antecedent to all its particular explicit formulations and is fertile and living, thus developing and unfolding throughout the ages.

(iii) The organ of tradition is the authority of the Church, that is, those who have authority in it.[24]

(iv) Tradition also exists, however, as actually expressed in what has already become a rule of faith (creed, *fides quae*), by the authority of faith. The question whether certain express affirmations were transmitted from the beginning side by side with scripture, whether, therefore, there is a second material principle besides scripture, independent from the beginning, becomes quite secondary in comparison; but it would probably have to be answered negatively.

e) The function of exegesis

In what has been said so far, it has almost exclusively been the limits of the letter of scripture, the freedom of the Spirit and the authority of the Church that have appeared. However, all the reflections that have been made also have a significance which points in the opposite direction, and which is related to the well-founded anxieties of Luther which we took as our starting-point. We have noted that revelation becomes present through preaching, and that preaching is interpretation; it is, therefore, possible and necessary to add the following.

Tradition by its very nature is always interpretation, does not exist independently, but only as exposition, interpretation "according to the scriptures". It is true even of the preaching of Jesus Christ himself that it appears as fulfilment, and consequently as interpretation, though of course as authoritative interpretation. It does not come with something absolutely new, never yet testified to in scripture, that is to say, in the Old Testament, but proclaims the reality of what was written and awakens this to a new life, which the mere historian was not in a position to derive from it. What holds good of Christ's message, that it assumed no other form than that of interpretation, emphatically holds good of the apostolic preaching and even more of the Church's preaching. As "tradition" it too must ultimately remain interpretation "according to the scriptures"; it must recognize that it is under an obligation to scripture and linked to it. It is true that it is not interpretation in the sense of purely exegetical exposition, but in virtue of the spiritual authority of the Lord operative in the whole existence of the Church, its faith, life and worship. But to a much greater extent than the Christ-event on which the Church is based, it remains interpretation tied to what has occurred and what has been spoken. In that way is expressed its link with

47

God's concrete action in this history and its unique historical character: the "once", which is just as essential to the reality of Christian revelation as the "forever". It is an expression of the unity of the Christ of faith and the Jesus of history; the Jesus of history is no other than the Christ of faith, even though faith is always more than history.

From this point of view it is clear that just as the Church has a task of vigilance linked with its charismatic bearing of witness, so too there is a duty of vigilance in the exegesis which investigates the literal sense, and so guards the link with the *sarx* of the Logos, in opposition to all *gnosis*. To that extent, therefore, there exists something like a certain independence of scripture as a separate, and in many respects perfectly un-ambiguous, criterion in face of the Church's magisterium. That was undoubtedly a correct insight on Luther's part, and in the Catholic Church not enough place has been accorded to it on account of the claims of the magisterium, the intrinsic limits of which have not always been sufficiently clearly perceived.

From this point of view something like a double criteriology in matters of faith has to be affirmed. On the one hand there is what the ancient Church called "the rule of faith", and with it the regulative function of the official witnesses as against scripture and its interpretation, that *praescriptio* of the rightful owner of scripture, and this, as Tertullian rightly noted, excludes any wilful playing off of scripture against the Church. On the other hand, however, there is also the limit set by the *littera scripturae,* the historically ascertainable literal meaning of scripture which, as we have said, certainly represents no absolute criterion subsisting in and for itself within the counterpoint of faith and knowledge, but does nevertheless represent a relatively independent criterion. What can be unambiguously recognized from scripture, whether by scientific methods or by simple reading, has the function of a real criterion, the test of which even the pronouncements of the magisterium itself have to meet. Certainly it is a question here of the lesser component, that of knowledge; it does not sit in judgment on faith, but it nevertheless continues to exist in faith as a critical court of appeal and as such has an urgent task, that of guarding the purity of the testimony *once* given, and of defending the *sarx* of history against the caprice of *gnosis* which perpetually seeks to establish its own autonomy.

At this point an important task accrues to the *reformatio* which the Church is striving with renewed earnestness to realize at the present historic hour. It may perhaps also open out new possibilities for the Church in its discussion with that struggle for *reformatio* which finally became a breach within western Christendom. Incorporated into the Church's authoritative ministry of giving testimony which draws its right and force from the presence of the Spirit and from Christ's perpetual presence, by which he is ever the Christ of today, the function of bearing witness, which belongs to the unique word of scripture set down once and for all, will have to be restored to its full rights and force. For that word derives its abiding validity from the unique character of the historical redemptive act of Jesus Christ, who once gave up his crucified body, himself, to the Father and so has perfected for all time those who are sanctified (cf. Heb 10:14; 7:27), he who is Christ yesterday and today and for ever (Heb 13:8).

III

ON THE INTERPRETATION OF
THE TRIDENTINE DECREE ON TRADITION

by

JOSEPH RATZINGER

The focussing of attention by Geiselmann on the reasons leading to the replacement of *partim-partim* by *et,* and the consequent concentration on a search for elements in the Tridentine discussions and their antecedents which seem to point to a material sufficiency of scripture, has resulted in undue narrowing of the inquiry. This to a large extent obscures the real background to the Tridentine decree.

1. *The pneumatological version of the concept of tradition in Cardinal Cervini's basic draft*

a) Contents

A detailed historical appreciation of the whole context of the problem would require an investigation no less far-reaching than Geiselmann undertook in his book.[1] That is beyond the scope of the present essay. All that can be done here is to recall a few facts of the Tridentine discussion, reflection on which could perhaps widen the horizons of the question again. The speech of the Cardinal Legate Cervini on 18 February 1546 seems to me fundamental to an understanding of the debate as well as of the decree finally decided on by the Council. The leading ideas of that speech are still clearly perceptible in the decree, just as they frequently are in other Tridentine decrees.[2] In addition it has the advantage of allowing the guiding principle to be much more clearly recognized than the decree itself, which was rendered less lucid by various compromises. As a supplementary aid to understanding the speech, there is also a letter addressed by the Cardinal Legates to Cardinal Alexander Farnese on 28 February 1546. It contains the same lines of thought—it was, of course, certainly inspired by Cervini—and throws additional light on certain points. Cervini explains in the speech that there are three principles and foundations of our faith:

1. The sacred books which were written under the inspiration of the Holy Spirit.

2. The gospel which our Lord did not write, but taught by word of mouth and implanted in men's hearts, and part of which the evangelists later wrote down, while much was simply entrusted to the hearts of the faithful.

3. Because the Son of God was not going to abide with us for ever physically, he sent the Holy Spirit, who was to reveal the mysteries of God in the hearts of the faithful and teach the Church all truth until the end of time.[3]

In a second, more detailed version of the speech, this line of thought was developed a little further. Revelation, we are told, has been made known differently at different times.

1. To the patriarchs, whose faith we have in the scriptures, and which we call the Old Testament.

2. In Christ, who implanted his gospel not in writing but orally, not *in charta* but *in corde*. Some of what derived from Christ (*quae e Christo emanarunt*) was written down, other things remained in the hearts of men (*quaedam in cordibus hominum relicta fuerunt*). This whole, the gospel of Christ, constituted in this double way, is, taken together, the *secundum principium fidei nostrae*, the Old Testament being the first.

3. There is a third principle as well (*tertium autem*), which consists of the following fact: Because the Son of man was not to remain with us always, he sent his Holy Spirit into the world; he was to reveal the mysteries of God and make clear anything which had remained doubtful in the minds of men.[4]

In a similar way, the above-mentioned letter to Cardinal Farnese speaks of two steps (*due passi*). One is that the revelation of our Lord was not all written down, but a part remained in the hearts of men and in the Church's tradition; the other step is to establish *quello che è suggerito lo Spirito Santo in la chiesa, maxime medianti i concilij, doppo l'ascensione in cielo del Signore*.[5]

We observe in the first place, therefore, that, contrary to our usual expectation and interpretation, not two but three principles are affirmed: scripture—gospel—revelation of the Spirit in the Church.

It is also important here that by "scripture" the Old Testament is meant, and that side by side with this, which is scripture in the proper sense, the gospel appears as a second principle. The Christ-event is included in the more comprehensive concept of "gospel", which itself includes what is written and what is inscribed in the hearts of the faithful. So the second principle itself indicates a pneumatic surplus over what is written: gospel in this view is something other than scripture and is, therefore, only partly written. (This must not be understood here in the sense, abhorred by Geiselmann, of a division of the contents of faith, but in the sense of an acknowledgement of its dignity: the gospel as such by its very nature can only partly be written.) Finally, and this is what to us is most astonishing, there follows a third principle, the revealing activity of the Holy Spirit throughout the age of the Church. We observe, therefore, that what we commonly call or think of as tradition does not appear here as *one* principle. Its basis is in fact divided between two contrasted principles: "gospel" as a principle which is always only partially transposable into scripture, and the operation of God's Spirit in the age of the Church. We can also observe that New Testament scripture does not appear as *one* principle side by side with apostolic tradition and even less (as is the case with us) does New Testament scripture, together with that of the Old Testament, comprise one single reality with which "tradition" might then be contrasted as a second reality. The New Testament complex of event and reality appears, taken as a unity, as a continuing double yet single principle, the gospel, and as such stands in contrast on the one hand to the Old Testament, on the other to the specific events of the subsequent age of the Church. Its inner unity is apparently stronger and more important than its division into written and unwritten, so that it can be contrasted as a single principle to the Old Testament, regardless of the two forms in which it is realized. The impossibility of designating the New Testament as scripture, which was so decisively felt by Paul and the early Christian centuries, is still plainly operative here.

The texts quoted also permit another observation. On neither of the bases of the concept of tradition which we have noted, that is to say, neither as regards the element in the second nor that in the third principle which points to tradition, does this appear as *verbal* tradition. In both cases it consists, rather, of a *real* tradition, as the surplus of reality over the word which bears witness to it. That should be self-evident as regards the third, pneumatological principle, but it is just as unmistakable in regard to the implanting of the gospel in men's hearts, of which the second principle speaks, and which extends beyond what is comprised in the scriptures.

The role that these ideas played in the Council's deliberations can also be seen from the *auctoritates* quoted in Cervini's presence. Among them were John 16:12 (. . . *Spiritus Sanctus suggeret* . . .) and Philippians 3:15 (*Quicumque perfecti sumus, haec sentiamus, et si quid aliter sentitis, haec quoque Deus vobis revelabit*), both of them passages very pneumatological in character, and bearing on the present.[6] That such ideas were not alien to the members of the Council is also clear from a number of other speeches. For instance, the Bishop of Aqui said that besides the holy scriptures there are some things in the Church of God which, transmitted from hand to hand, have come down to us from the apostles, as well as many other things *quae etsi scripta apostoli nobis non reliquerunt, per Spiritus Sancti revelationem nobis (tradita) sunt (tradita* is a correction, replacing *revelata*).[7] On this basis tradition might even be described as the pneumatological component of the Christ-event.

b) The influence of the draft on various Council decrees

It is, of course, true that this triple conception is very faint in the official decree on tradition. But it is clear from two other texts of the Council that it was not abandoned in essentials, for these make use *in actu*, as it were, of the realities in question.[8] So, for example, we read in the introduction to the decree on the Eucharist (*Denzinger* 873a: . . . *sacrosancta synodus, sanam . . . doctrinam tradens, quam semper catholica Ecclesia ab ipso Iesu Christo Domino nostro et eius Apostolis erudita, atque a Spiritu Sancto illi omnem veritatem in dies suggerente* (John 14:16) *edocta retinuit . . . .*

Here the actual activity of the Council is described as *tradere* and a double background given to this *tradere*. On the one hand there is instruction by Jesus and the apostles. This corresponds to Cervini's concept of the gospel, and by the mention of Jesus as well as the apostles it displays to some extent the double form taken by the original testimony, at once written and implanted in men's hearts. On the other hand there is instruction by the Holy Spirit who *"in dies"*, in time as it moves onwards, leads into truth.

The other text to which we can refer here comes in the preamble to the doctrine on Purgatory (*Denzinger* 983) which reads: . . . *catholica Ecclesia, Spiritu Sancto edocta, ex sacris Litteris et antiqua Patrum traditione in sacris Conciliis et novissime in hac . . . Synodo docuerit.* The description of the Council's own activity as *tradere* is, for that matter, also found in the declarations about the sacrament of order (*Denzinger* 910).

Finally, the threefold conception can be discovered in the background of the decree on tradition itself, even though it is obscured and weakened by all kinds of insertions intended as supplements or in the service of other themes.

1. The decree speaks of the gospel promised through the prophets in the holy scriptures. By this it attaches the term holy scripture in the narrower sense to the Old Testament.

2. Mention is made of the promulgation of the gospel by Christ, and of its transmission by the apostles in double form, orally and in writing. And here (but not in Cervini) the pneumatological element appears united to the apostolic, because two kinds of apostolic traditions are distinguished, those which derive from Christ and those which derive from the inspiration of the Holy Spirit. It is clear that, as compared with Cervini's draft, we are in the presence of a certain insistence on history, which strengthens the link with the historical beginning and at the same time seems to transfer the emphasis from real tradition to verbal tradition.

3. The part of the decree on tradition, which has just been analysed, is followed once again by an examination of the concept of sacred scripture and only then is the concept of tradition finally given definitive formulation. Tradition is now described as *vel oretenus a Christo vel a Spiritu Sancto dictatas et continua successione in Ecclesia catholica conservatas*. The reference to the apostles is now lacking; the entire piece can, of course, be regarded as a reference back to what preceded, and it can be said that what are meant are traditions already dictated to the apostles and then handed on, and the addition

of *continua successio* even suggests this interpretation. Yet a certain indefiniteness remains which still leaves open the possibility of finding traces of Cervini's third component, the real pneumatic principle. It is, of course, also clear that this conception has receded into the background and that an attempt was made at agreement with a conception that was more strongly historical in character.

In view of all this, the question inescapably arises what in fact was really meant by the pneumatological conception; and especially how the idea—a surprising one for us—of continuing *revelatio* can be given an intelligible meaning[9] in view of the uniqueness and historical links of revelation, of which, of course, Cervini was perfectly aware, as was the patristic and mediaeval tradition that stands behind him. Before we attempt to answer this question, a brief consideration must be devoted to explaining what the themes (chiefly supplementary ones) were which entered into the Tridentine decree on scripture and tradition, and, as has been said, partly overlaid Cervini's conception. Above all it must be asked what theological intentions prevailed here, though, of course, in a text which was composed as a compromise between several originally very divergent views, they could find only imperfect expression. A detailed discussion would once again exceed the limits of this essay; a few summary remarks must suffice.

2. *The connection between tradition and the life of the Church in various contributions to the Tridentine debates*

A first group of themes under which a number of speeches can be classified, however different their outward tenor, is shown in the idea which left its mark on the decree in the two formulas: (a) *per manus traditae ad nos usque pervenerunt* and (b) *continua successione in Ecclesia catholica conservatas.*

What lies behind these two formulas which, for the historian of the present day, are so difficult to digest, precisely because of their supposed historical emphasis? It may be said that a decisive role was played here by the idea, which was frequently urged in the discussion, that traditions are changeable, that so much that was apostolic has been abolished, and that on the other hand ecclesiastical traditions have supervened which should not be abandoned.[10] The conception of tradition operative in this line of thought is clear, for example, in the treatise on tradition composed for the Council Fathers by Seripando. In this, Seripando speaks of written traditions contained in holy scripture, such as St James's proviso, the veiling of women, marriage legislation in I Corinthians 7, and other similar things. He points out that many such things have been abrogated and concludes that, although they are close to the word of God, they are only "remotely close", for nothing may be taken from the word of God. With these he contrasts the traditions which are not contained in the Bible. These are partly apostolic or owed their origin to General Councils and were observed by the whole Church, and partly local traditions and, therefore, subject to change.[11]

This text leads to a surprising conclusion: for Seripando (and for many other Fathers at Trent)[12] there are traditions *in* scripture. "Tradition " is not what is unwritten, but is found in scripture and outside it. That leads to the further question: What actually constitutes the nature of tradition for the said Fathers, if being unwritten does not?[13] Or, to put it in another way, how must tradition positively be defined, if it cannot adequately be determined by the negative idea of being unwritten?

There are a number of pointers to the answer. Seripando himself gives the following definition: *Traditiones, hoc est apostolorum seu sanctorum patrum sanctae et salutares constitutiones.*[14] A clearer answer to our question is offered by a statement of Cervini which Massarelli reports. To the objection of the Bishop of Chioggia, who quoted the supposed remark of Augustine that everything necessary for salvation is written, Cervini gave the following answer: *Verba illa* (i.e. of St Augustine) *formaliter intelligi debent, scilicet ad fidem accipiendam, ut salvi fiamus. Quo vero ad mores et christianam vitam instituendam certe non omnia scripta sunt.* And Cervini again refers to John 15:26 and 14:26 and so alludes to the pneumatological factor.[15] What is really meant should stand out quite clearly here: Tradition refers to the *institutio vitae,* to the mode of realization of the word in actual Christian living. In other words, it is the form in which the word finds reality and without which the word would remain unreal.

Two other groups of speeches lead to the same conclusion. It is one of the striking things about the Council discussion which, of course, is understandable in view of the situation described above, in the introduction to the previous chapter, that the dogmatic discussion of the concept of tradition was continually overshadowed by the question of procedure: Should the *reformatio,* the practical reform of the Church, be dealt with first (as the emperor wished), or the dogmatic questions discussed first (as the pope wished)?[16] In itself, that was a question of procedure, and although it perpetually

59

cropped up in the debate, it did not directly concern the conception of tradition as such. But the way in which it was in fact linked to the question of tradition itself is nevertheless very striking, and with some speakers the question of procedure (whether abuses or tradition were to be dealt with) became part of their argument in the substantial problem itself.[17] In that way the problem of abuses and the problem of tradition became linked in fact, and appeared as fundamentally a single question, simply assuming a positive or negative form as the case might be. That, of course, did in fact correspond to the Reformation point of view, according to which the *traditiones* were the *abusus* which deformed the Church. The Fathers clearly felt this and were conscious that by defending the traditions, they were ultimately defending the *usus ecclesiae,* the way in which the Church in the concrete actually accomplished its life.

The other series of pronouncements pointing in the same direction is found in those statements which emphasized the *auctoritas* of the Church as decisive, and so in their way spoke for a closer relation of tradition and *institutio christiana*.[18]

This permits us to return to the starting-point of this circular line of thought, and answer the question what the formula *ad nos usque pervenerunt* actually means. Objectively speaking, the intention was certainly not to define an historical viewpoint, which the formula may appear to our ears to express, but the Church's insistence on the reality of the *institutio vitae christianae*, the form of human existence actually current and valid in the Church's present, and which alone provides for scripture the place where it assumes reality. As such, that is to say, as something which is living and which is more extensive than scripture, it is fundamentally apostolic, though in details it is, of course, changeable like everything living.

3. Tradition and the Church's dogma

A second group of themes left its mark on the decree in the formula *traditiones tum ad fidem tum ad mores pertinentes.* For although in what has so far been said, the idea of tradition appears to a large extent restricted to what the Fathers of the Council called *consuetudines, observationes, institutiones*, the procurator of the Cardinal of Augsburg, Claude Lejay, SJ, in particular made himself the spokesman of the view which emphasized the importance of tradition concerning faith, as distinct from the *traditiones caeremoniales*. The treatise on tradition which he, too, composed for the information of the Fathers, contains the formula subsequently adopted by the Council: *Denique multas veritates tum ad fidem tum ad mores pertinentes Ecclesia novit, quas scriptura aperte et expresse non continet.* As examples he quotes the words *persona, essentia, trinitas*, from the doctrine of the Trinity; *consubstantialitas* from Logos-Christology; two natures, one person from the dogma of Chalcedon. He also lists: Christ as Mary's only son, two natures in one person in Christ, a rational soul as well as the divine mind in Christ, Anne as Mary's mother, use of the sign of the Cross, Sunday observance, turning to the east to pray—that is to say, ideas and facts of conciliar tradition and of the tradition of piety.[19] Cervini, who immediately took up[20] Lejay's speech, on 23 February 1546, had no difficulty in linking this line of thought with his own, as expressed in the

letter to Cardinal Farnese already mentioned, where, as we
have seen, it is said that the Holy Spirit has spoken in the
Church and, since our Lord's ascension, speaks *maxime
mediante i concilij.*[21] He obviously thought that in that speech
the fact was rightly emphasized that the surplus which is
represented by the living Church, as compared with the merely
written word, concerned, and concerns, not simply the *vita
instituenda* or, as he puts it in this context, the *caeremonialia,*
but also the *essentialia fidei* which find full expression only in
tradition. Here too then, as can be seen, the dominant interest
lies not in an historical idea of transmission from the beginning, but rather in the view that the fact of tradition, operative
chiefly through the conciliar practice of the Church, is of
fundamental importance for *fides*, too, for the doctrine which
is believed, not simply for pious practice, the *"caeremonialia"*.

4. *The meaning of the Tridentine decree*

In view of what has been considered so far, it can be said
that it is possible without much difficulty to perceive three
different theological conceptions which were brought together
in the final text of the decree on tradition. They were not
brought into exact agreement, but to some extent were simply
juxtaposed, despite their considerable differences. Nevertheless
they were linked by the fundamental tendency which they
have in common.

1. Cervini's conception, which we termed the pneumatological
one. With its doctrine of the three *principia fidei*, it laid stress
on the dynamic character of the Christ-reality present in the

Church, and so understood tradition primarily as the reality of the *institutio vitae christianae* under the guidance of the Holy Spirit.

2. The conception which we may call the ceremonial one. This regarded tradition essentially as the domain (parallel to *fides*) of *consuetudines*, as the *usus ecclesiae* which the Reformers wrongly attempted to reject as *abusus*. This conception was concerned to defend the antiquity and apostolic dignity of traditions; its idea was restricted by the *ad nos usque pervenerunt*, which expresses the idea of variation which makes a limitation necessary. In the *pervenire* and *conservare*, the idea of acceptance by the Church is expressed and, together with antiquity, is made a supplementary criterion.

3. The conception which we might perhaps call the dogmatic one. As opposed to an identification of the concept of tradition with the domain of *consuetudo*, it emphasized the fact that the phenomenon of *traditio* extends to the domain of *fides* also.

These three conceptions shaped the text, and quite clearly in such a way that its guiding line derives from Cervini; the whole text must be understood against the background of Cervini's idea. The second of these conceptions was, however, included in two insertions, the . . . *pervenerunt* and . . . *conservatas*, while the third conception was introduced in the *tum ad fidem tum ad mores*.

As opposed to these three conceptions, of which there were, of course, a number of variants, but which nevertheless taken together expressed the really leading ideas which prevailed, the position of Bonuccio and Nacchianti, which Geiselmann stresses so much, appears as one of mere opposition. Bonuccio's objection obviously referred more to the second conception, and was aimed against over-valuing *consuetudines*—not to be received *par pietatis affectus*. Nacchianti's opposition was primarily directed to the third conception and emphasized the adequate character of the transmission of faith by scripture.[22]

It should finally be added that conceptions two and three have the common feature that they set against Cervini's pneumatological perspective, based on the perpetual presence of salvation, a more historical view, centred on the transmission of what is unique, focussed that is to say, on the ἐφάπαξ. In fact it must be said that both Cervini's view, with its focus on the present, and the more historical perspective of the other groups, would each, taken separately, have been dangerous if not untenable, but that, taken together, their respective differences and mutual limitation make a correct view possible. In the present text, both points of view are represented, though not in any detail, both the factor that concerns the present and that of the ἐφάπαξ. It is well to understand the text as requiring precisely that we should regard both elements as essential and so recognize that both go to constitute the Christian reality, and even that part of it which we call tradition—both the presence of the Spirit and the link with the unique events that once occurred in history.

In this way there finally appears the answer to the question of how we are to understand the view of the Council of Trent as a whole. The first and most important fact seems to me to be that the Council still very clearly perceived the connection of the concept of tradition with that of revelation. This in turn is connected with the fact that, in accordance with patristic and mediaeval tradition, it still conceived the notion of revelation in a far less material way than was subsequently the case. Only in that way is the idea of the revelation of the Holy Spirit in the Church to be understood. From the point of view of the branch of mediaeval theology, strongly marked by patristic influence, which still persisted in fact in Cervini's speeches, the thesis that revelation closed with the death of the last apostle must have appeared far too unqualified. This question cannot, of course, be gone into in detail here. It would be possible in fact to formulate the solution of the question, as it was then envisaged, with the help of present-day categories and say that, according to the theology in question, revelation is indeed closed as regards its material principle, but is present and remains as regards its reality. To put it another way: we are dealing with a view in which revelation certainly has its ἐφάπαξ, to the extent that it was accomplished in historical facts, but has also its perpetual reality today, because what was once accomplished remains perpetually living and effective in the faith of the Church, and Christian faith never simply refers to what is past but equally to what is present and to what is to come. The later emphasis on the historical and material character of the concept of revelation is, of course, clearly anticipated in the Tridentine debates themselves, but was not yet a fully accomplished fact, even if it must perhaps be admitted that in the compromises of the Council a decisive contribution was made to its eventual success. We may finally add that, according to what we have said, four strata in all of the concept of tradition can be discerned in the Tridentine debates:

1. The inscription of revelation — the gospel, not simply in the Bible but in men's hearts;

2. the Holy Spirit speaking throughout the whole age of the Church;

3. the conciliar activity of the Church;

4. liturgical tradition and the whole tradition of the Church's life.

In these four strata, which must be borne in mind as the conceptual background of the decree, there is expressed the one reality of the Christian present, in which, of course, the whole post-apostolic past of the Church (which in fact reaches back into the apostolic period itself) is also present as the totality of the Church's life, in which scripture is a central, but never the only, element. By and large, it should have become clear that despite—or even precisely because of—the lack of exact harmony and the incompleteness of its conception, Trent presents a much richer testimony than was perceived during the centuries that followed, so that theological work today, with its new insight, can receive from it new stimulus, confirmation and guidance in its endeavours.

APPENDIX

Summary of the Composition of the Tridentine Decree on Tradition

First principle according to Cervini:
(Old Testament = scripture)

Sacrosancta oecumenica et generalis Tridentina Synodus, in Spiritu Sancto legitime congregata, . . . hoc sibi perpetuo ante oculos proponens, ut sublatis erroribus puritas ipsa EVANGELII in Ecclesia conservetur, quod PROMISSUM ANTE PER PROPHETAS IN SCRIPTURIS SANCTIS

Second principle according to Cervini: Gospel partly written, partly implanted in men's hearts.

DOMINUS NOSTER JESUS CHRISTUS DEI FILIUS PROPRIO ORE PRIMUM PROMULGAVIT, DEINDE PER SUOS APOSTOLOS TAMQUAM FONTEM OMNIS ET SALUTARIS VERITATIS ET MORUM DISCIPLINAE "OMNI CREATURAE PRAEDICARI" (Mc 16:15) IUSSIT; PERSPICIENSQUE HANC VERITATEM CONTINERI IN LIBRIS SCRIPTIS ET SINE SCRIPTO TRADITIONIBUS, QUAE AB IPSIUS CHRISTI ORE AB APOSTOLIS ACCEPTAE, AUT AB IPSIS APOSTOLIS SPIRITU SANCTO DICTANTE

Seripando, Cervini and others: Only traditions received by the Church (*ad nos usque* . . .) are meant.

quasi per manus traditae ad nos usque pervenerunt,

orthodoxorum Patrum exempla secuta, omnes libros tam Veteris quam Novi testamenti, cum utriusque unus Deus sit auctor, nec non TRADITIONES IPSAS, tum ad fidem, tum ad mores pertinentes,

Lejay: Tradition referring not only to *consuetudo* but also to *fides* (conciliar formulas!).

Cervini's third principle: After Christ's ascension, the Holy Spirit declares the mysteries of God.

TAMQUAM VEL ORETENUS A CHRISTO, VEL A SPIRITU SANCTO DICTATAS

Seripando, Cervini, etc.: Only what is received permanently by the Church is meant (as above).

et continua successione in ecclesia catholica conservatas,

Cervini:
Scripture and tradition both deriving from the same Holy Spirit.

pari pietatis affectu ac reverentia suscepit et veneratur. . .

NOTES

CHAPTER I

[1] On the difference between non-biblical and Old Testament revelation history (which persists even on the assumption that there is a non-biblical history of revelation), see K. Rahner, *Schriften zur Theologie,* vol. V (1964), pp. 136-58, especially pp. 148 f. and 153 f.

CHAPTER II

[1] That is clear from the lists of *traditiones* drawn up at the time of the Council of Trent; cf. the material indicated below, chapter III, note 19.

[2] Art. 28, 39-42 in *Die Bekenntnisschriften der evangelisch-lutherischen Kirche* (²1952), pp. 126 f.

[3] Art 28, 52, ibid., p. 129.

[4] Ibid., p. 463 f.

[5] Art. 7, 1, ibid., p. 61.

[6] Cf. on this and on what follows J. Ratzinger, "Das geistliche Amt und die Einheit der Kirche" in *Catholica* 17 (1963), pp. 165-79.

[7] References in chapter III, notes 16 and 17.

[8] Published in E. Peterson, *Theologische Traktate* (1951), pp. 295 f.

[9] Cf. the report of R. Laurentin, *L'enjeu du Concile. Bilan de la première session* (1963), pp. 27-45; Y. Congar, *Vatican II. Le concile*

au jour le jour (1963), pp. 63–71, E.T.: *Report from Rome on the First Session of the Vatican Council* (1964); J. Ratzinger, *Die erste Sitzungsperiode des Zweiten Vatikanischen Konzils* (1963), pp. 38–50.

[10] See above all his synoptic account: J. R. Geiselmann, *Die Heilige Schrift und die Tradition* (1962), especially pp. 91–107 and 274–82. Among the earlier works of Geiselmann on the same theme, one is of particular importance: "Das Konzil von Trient über das Verhältnis der Heiligen Schrift und der nichtgeschriebenen Traditionen" in M. Schmaus, ed., *Die mündliche Überlieferung* (1957), pp. 123–206.

[11] A summary of all those who have agreed in principle with Geiselmann is given by H. Küng in his article "Karl Barths Lehre vom Wort Gottes als Frage an die katholische Theologie" in J. Ratzinger and H. Fries, ed., *Einsicht und Glaube,* (²1963), p. 105, note 25.

[12] This statement is not meant in a sense that would make scripture simply an unsubstantial report of facts which remain entirely external to it. On the contrary, it should remain abundantly clear (as we hope what follows will show) that the reality of revelation is a word-reality, that in the word of preaching the reality of revelation comes to the individual human being. The fact remains, however, that the mere presence of the word of scripture is not the reality of revelation itself, which is never simply "there". The above remark is simply meant to draw attention to the difference between scripture and the reality which makes itself known in scripture, a difference which is not annulled by the verbal character of revelation.

[13] Cf. G. Gloege, "Schriftprinzip" in *Die Religion in Geschichte und Gegenwart,* vol. V (³1961), col. 1540–3, with bibliography. On the concept of revelation, cf. M. Vereno, R. Schnackenburg and H. Fries in *Lexikon für Theologie und Kirche,* vol. VII (²1962), col. 1104–15; J. R. Geiselmann, "Offenbarung" in H. Fries, *Handbuch theologischer Grundbegriffe,* vol. II (1963), pp. 242–50 and bibliography.

[14] Cf. W. H. van de Pol, *Das reformatorische Christentum* (1956), pp. 117–92.

[15] Cf. on this point the important article ἀποχαλύπτω of A. Oepke in *Theologisches Wörterbuch zum Neuen Testament,* vol. III (1938), pp. 565–97.

[16] See on this the valuable remarks of G. Schrenk in his article γραφή-γράμμα in *Theologisches Wörterbuch zum Neuen Testament*, vol. I (1933), pp. 749–69, especially pp. 767 ff.

[17] Cf., for example, the account given by G. v. Rad, *Theologie des Alten Testamentes*, vol. II (1960), pp. 402–24.

[18] H. Schlier, "Die Kirche nach dem Brief an die Epheser" in *Die Zeit der Kirche* ([3]1962), pp. 159–86.

[19] On this account of the matter, see the observations of E. Peterson which are still fundamental: "Die Kirche" in *Theologische Traktate* (1951), pp. 409–29; H. Schlier, "Die Entscheidung für die Heidenmission in der Urchristenheit" in *Die Zeit der Kirche*, pp. 90–107. It seems to me certain that both the analysis of the synoptic tradition regarding Jesus's message and its eschatological orientation, and an examination of the earliest Christian history by means of the material contained in the Acts of the Apostles, allow of no other solution of the problem of the relation between the message of the kingdom and the Church's preaching than this. It in no way follows from this, in my opinion, as is often feared, that the significance of the Cross is changed into an accident of secondary importance, which really could have been avoided. On the contrary, the crucifixion-structure of the Church becomes even more radical, because only in this way do the serious reality of human freedom and the gravity of Christ's passion, as well as the total origin of the Church from the Cross, receive their full weight.

[20] Cf. H. Gross, "Motivtransposition als Form- und Traditionsprinzip im Alten Testament" in H. Vorgrimler, ed., *Exegese und Dogmatik* (1962), pp. 134–52 and bibliography, E.T.: "Transposition of Themes as Principal of Form and Tradition in the Old Testament" in *Dogmatic versus Biblical Theology* (1964); G. v. Rad, op. cit., vol. II, pp. 332–9 and 396–401.

[21] The non-identity of these two theologies of the Old Testament has been emphasized very harshly by R. Bultmann, "Weissagung und Erfüllung" in *Glauben und Verstehen*, vol. II (1952), pp. 162–86; the necessary qualifications to this, in which the historical basis for what systematic theology calls *analogia fidei* is made clear, can be found in

71

G. v. Rad, op. cit., vol. II, pp. 329-424, especially p. 420, note 25, and p. 422, note 29. On the theme of the *analogia fidei* between the two testaments, see also E. Przywara, *Alter und Neuer Bund* (1956).

[22] Cf., for example, the instructive account in G. Bornkamm, *Jesus von Nazareth* (1956), E.T.: *Jesus of Nazareth* (1960). On the question touched upon here, see H. Schlier, "Über Sinn und Aufgabe einer Theologie des Neuen Testamentes" (E.T.: "The Meaning and Function of a Theology of the New Testament") in H. Vorgrimler, op. cit., pp. 69-90.

[23] On this question the best that has been said as regards the Fathers will still be found in A. v. Harnack, *Lehrbuch der Dogmengeschichte,* vol. II ([5]1931), pp. 84-116. Harnack actually says, p. 87, note 3: "The 'Canon' was originally the rule of faith; scripture has in truth intervened, yet in such a way that its authority had a significance lying still further back, namely, in the Old Testament and the words of the Lord". I have tried to show that this was still true in the Middle Ages, and that here (together with the concept of *revelatio,* which will be dealt with in the next chapter) the placing of "*fides*" (the creed) higher than *scriptura* represents the essential form of the idea of tradition. See my essay: "Wesen und Weisen der auctoritas im Werk des heiligen Bonaventura" in Corsten, Frotz and Linden, ed., *Die Kirche und ihre Ämter und Stände, Festgabe Kardinal Frings* (1960), pp. 58-72.

[24] This line of thought cannot be developed in greater detail here, as it would really require to be, for we are only concerned to indicate the basis of the concept of tradition. In view of the limitation of the theme, I have been content in the preceding theses to develop the matter to the point where it becomes evident that tradition is concerned with the "Church" (cf. theses 4 and 5). What that means could only be explained in more precise terms by an analysis of the concept of the Church, which must be taken for granted here. Cf. my article on ministry and unity of the Church mentioned in note 6 above; in it I attempted a few observations on the matter.

CHAPTER III

NOTE: *CT* has been used below as abbreviation of *Concilium Tridentinum* (1901 ff.).

[1] Unfortunately Geiselmann obtained his account of the mediaeval situation at second hand, so that its historical value is questionable. See my remarks in the *Theologisch-praktische Quartalschrift* (1963), pp. 224–7. They are not affected by the vivacity of Geiselmann's reactions in *Tübinger Theologische Quartalschrift* 144 (1964), pp. 31–69, which can scarcely be described as contributing to advance the discussion. A valuable account is given by Y. Congar, *La tradition et les traditions. Essai historique* (1960), E.T.: *Tradition and Traditions, An Historical Essay* (1966); also important is J. Beumer, *Die mündliche Überlieferung als Glaubensquelle* (1962). On Trent, besides the fundamental work of Jedin, see especially E. Ortigues, "Ecriture et Traditions apostoliques au Concile de Trente" in *Recherches de science religieuse* 36 (1949), pp. 271–99; K. D. Schmidt, *Studien zur Geschichte des Konzils von Trient* (1925), pp. 152–209.

[2] The speech has been handed down in two versions, a shorter one in the *Acta* in *CT*, vol. V, p. 11, and a longer one in Massarelli's diary (*Diarium* III) in *CT*, vol. I, pp. 484 f. The two versions are, however, identical in content. In the following analysis the two versions will be presented successively. On Cervini's position at the Council, see H. Jedin, *Geschichte des Konzils von Trient*, vol. II (1957), pp. 38–40, E.T.: *A History of the Council of Trent* (2 vols., 1957-1961). The account of the historical course of the discussion in Jedin, pp. 42–82, may be assumed here as the background of the theological analysis.

[3] *CT*, vol. V, p. 11 ". . . tria esse principia et fundamenta nostrae fidei: primum libros sacros . . ., secundum esse evangelium, quod Christus Dominus Noster non scripsit, sed ore docuit et in cordibus illud plantavit, cuius evangelii nonnulla evangelistae scripto mandarunt, multa quoque relicta sunt in cordibus hominum. Tertium, quia non semper filius Dei corporaliter nobiscum mansurus erat, misit Spiritum Sanctum, qui in cordibus fidelium secreta Dei revelaret et ecclesiam

quotidie et usque ad consummationem saeculi doceret omnem veritatem, et si quid in mentibus hominum dubii occurrisset, declararet".

[4] *CT*, vol. I, p. 484. The formula used on p. 485, lines 14–16 is also noteworthy: "Nihil tamen inter scripturas sacras et apostolicas traditiones differt; illae enim scriptae, hae per insinuationem habentur, utraeque tamen a spiritu sancto eodem modo emanatae". Similarly *CT*, vol. V, p. 11, line 19: ". . . ab eodem spiritu et illos (sc. libros) et istas (sc. traditiones) descendisse".

[5] *CT*, vol. X, p. 373.

[6] *CT*, vol. V, pp. 14 and 15. Investigation of all the scriptural and patristic *auctoritates*, which appear in this collection as testimonies to the reality of tradition, would itself be informative for what was understood by tradition. H. Holstein has devoted a noteworthy study to it: "La tradition d'après le Concile de Trente" in *Recherches de science religieuse* 47 (1959), pp. 367–90. In the texts he finds two main tendencies. There is the Irenaeus line, for which the testimony of the apostles is the testimony of their personality, life and office. There is also the line of Tertullian—Cyprian—Basil—Augustine, which might be called the "ceremonial" line. Origen belongs, he thinks, to both. In fact in this collection of quotations there is a series of texts referring to *observationes, consuetudines, institutiones,* which suggest that tradition is to be found in that direction. But there are also texts which emphasize that the gospel is written in the hearts of the faithful. And there are regularly those which point out that the Church is the place where Christ's truth is found.

[7] *CT*, vol. I, p. 483 (18 February 1546). We find Cervini returning to this statement on 26 February (*CT*, vol. V, p. 18). Cf. also a pronouncement of the Bishop of Fano, *CT*, vol. V, p. 10: "Cum iam receperimus scripturas sacras, necessario recipiendae sunt traditiones, quae ab eodem Spiritu Sancto quo scripturae dictatae sunt . . ."

[8] My attention was first drawn to this by a study of C. H. R. Limbach prepared under my direction, to which I also owe other references.

[9] I have attempted a short sketch on that background in my article "Offenbarung — Schrift — Überlieferung" in *Trierer Theologische Zeitschrift* 67 (1958), pp. 13–27; cf. also J. Beumer, "Der theoretische Beitrag der Frühscholastik zum Problem des Dogmenfortschritts" in

Zeitschrift für katholische Theologie 72 (1952), pp. 205-26; J. de Ghellinck, "Pour l'histoire du mot 'revelare'" in *Recherches de science religieuse* 6 (1916), pp. 149-57.

[10] Here is the place of a statement of Cervini on 26 February 1546, reported in *CT,* vol. I, p. 33, and vol. V, p. 18, that not all traditions which go back to the apostles are to be accepted, but only those which "ab ecclesia receptae ad nos usque pervenerunt" (vol. V, p. 18). This statement, which anticipates the phrasing of the conciliar dogma, can at the same time be taken as an authentic commentary of this difficult formula, in which, therefore, it is essentially a matter of stressing the *receptio ecclesiae.* Under the date 23 March a statement of the Bishop of Bertinoro is reported (vol. I. pp. 523 f.), in which he stressed that the written traditions have in part been changed, that among the unwritten traditions there are those that have been changed and those that have not (admixture of water in the wine, chrism, auricular confession) and that finally quite unchangeable things belong there, such as *descensus ad inferos,* Mary's perpetual virginity, the replacement of the Sabbath by Sunday. Other matters had been preserved in the East but changed in the West. A statement of the Bishop of Bitonto dated 27 March is reported (vol. I, p. 39), expressing the view that some things were handed on by the apostles for perpetual keeping (such as what belongs to *fides*), some things have ceased (St James's precept), some things were meant as counsel. In a similar way, of course, some things were written in scripture which were not observed because they were only counselled: "If any one would sue you and take your coat, let him have your cloak as well; if any one strikes you on the right cheek, turn to him the other also"—certainly rather a remarkable solution of the problem of the Sermon on the Mount. Finally, similar ideas are also found in Lejay, for instance in the speech of 23 February (*CT,* vol. V, p. 13), where we read: "Nam illae (sc. traditiones), quae ad fidem pertinent, eadem sunt recipiendae auctoritate qua recipitur evangelium, alia autem non ita, cum earum plurimae immutatae fuerint, ut de bigamis, de esu sanguinis et similia". For that matter we also find Bonuccio, vol. I, p. 525 (23 March 1546) saying: ". . . ecclesia traditiones apostolorum quandoque mutavit, verbum autem Dei numquam mutavit neque mutare potest . . ."

[11] Seripando, *De traditionibus* (February or March 1546), *CT,* vol. XII,

pp. 517–21 and in particular p. 521. In content the last thought is close to Cervini's idea of the *receptio ecclesiae*.

[12] Cf. the texts referred to in note 11.

[13] As a matter of fact this idea no longer appears in the text of the decree, where when tradition is first mentioned, the antithesis is at once set up "in libris scriptis et sine scripto traditionibus". The second mention is not so exclusive, but has the same tendency by its contrast with "omnes libros . . . nec non traditiones ipsas". Yet the positive conception of tradition, which forms the background of this discussion, was not without influence even on the decree.

[14] *CT,* vol. XII, p. 517.

[15] *CT,* vol. I, pp. 494 f. (26 February 1546). The supposed saying of St Augustine played a part in the discussion in another matter also. Seripando refers to it as follows (*De traditionibus, CT,* vol. XII, p. 521, lines 47–53): "Pensandum denique, ne in traditionibus externis vera religio et salutis spes statuatur, de quibus Augustinus: Omnia, quae pertinent ad veram religionem quaerendam et tenendam, divina Scriptura non tacuit". Not everything is written down, of course (John 21:25!), "electa sunt autem, quae scriberentur, quae saluti credentium sufficere videbantur". More than anywhere else in the Tridentine debate the real concern of the Reformers is grasped here: it is not exterior practices which save; what is decisive for salvation is encountered in the word of scripture. The "sufficiency" of scripture that is spoken of here is, of course, something different from the material sufficiency asserted by Geiselmann and of much more radical significance. Unfortunately it has not yet been possible to identify Augustine's text (*CT,* vol. I, p. 494 suggests *De doctrina christiana* II, 9 and *De peccatorum meritis et remissione* II, 59). Instructive in this connection are the references of H. Schauf, "Schrift und Tradition" in *Antonianum* 39 (1964), pp. 200–9, to the so-called Düsseldorf religious discussion. In the texts presented by Schauf, the sufficiency of scripture for salvation is asserted with the same reference to Augustine, but its sufficiency for the order of the whole Church is nevertheless contested. In fact such an alternative appears to be much more meaningful and, from the point of view of the intention of the Reformers, much more fundamental than the alternative of material sufficiency or insufficiency of scripture.

[16] On the dispute about questions of procedure, Jedin, op. cit., pp. 9–82, should again be consulted.

[17] So, for example, in Cervini's great speech which is analysed at the beginning (*CT,* vol. I, p. 484), and in which Cervini presents the dilemma of the Council: if it turns to the *traditiones,* the Fathers would be surprised: "quasi reformationem fugiamus; si ipsam reformationem sumimus, iterum obiicient, traditiones relinquendas non esse . . ." The conclusion is similar in two interventions of the Bishop of Astorga, 23 February 1546, *CT,* vol. V, pp. 13 and 19, in Seripando (vol. I, p. 484: ". . . traditiones prius pertractandas consulit; tantam enim conformitatem abusus, qui ex sacris libris descendunt, cum iis, qui a traditionibus orti sunt, habent, ut sacris libris et traditionibus absolutis duo illa abusuum genera simul pertractari valeant") and Bonuccio (vol. I, p. 484: In the first place they were to deal with the scriptures, the apostolic canons, the General Councils and the papal decretals. "Hisque susceptis ad abusus ex eisdem dependentes devenire").

[18] That is particularly clear with Alfons de Castro, *CT,* vol. I, p. 484: "Quoniam ultra traditiones apostolicas ecclesiae auctoritatem habemus, quae ecclesiae auctoritas tanta apud nos est, ut aliqui eam maioris roboris quam sacros libros esse sentiant . . ." Similarly vol. I, p. 491, lines 45 f. In substance a number of Lejay's pronouncements follow the same line, especially *CT,* vol. XII, p. 524 (Treatise *De traditionibus ecclesiae,* February or March 1546).

[19] *CT,* vol. XII, p. 523. Lejay obviously bases himself here on lists of traditions of which a number were drawn up at that time, for example, by Eck, Driedo, Cano, Soto and Nogarola. Cf. on this Y. Congar, "Traditions apostoliques non écrites et suffisance de l'Ecriture" in *Istina* 6 (1959), pp. 219–306, especially pp. 289 ff.

[20] *CT,* vol. V, p. 14.

[21] *CT,* vol. X, p. 373.

[22] In any case it seems clear from a statement of Cervini that the Bishop of Chioggia finally abandoned his thesis of the sufficiency of scripture, which met with general opposition. In Cervini's letter to Cardinal Farnese of 27 February 1546 we read: ". . . Chioggia, che (quasi quasi) voleva dire queste traditioni essere superflue, perorando, che tutto quello che era necessario alla salute era scritto, et allegando etiam S.

Agostino sopra l'ultimo capitulo di S. Giovanni a questo proposito. Pure, per non poter negare, che molte cose, appartenenti almeno alli sacramenti, non ci fussero venute ex traditione, et per consequente, che non tutte le cose necessarie alla nostra salute erano scritte, poichè ebbe fatte molte distintioni, concluse, che ancor lui accettava queste 'che in la chiesa fusse qualche traditione apostolica non scritta'; (et con queste parole diceva, che se ne facesse il decreto); credo che molti sono restati scandalizati di lui" (*CT*, vol. X, no. 315, p. 399, lines 4–11). Cf. also *CT*, vol. I, p. 494, note 9, and p. 495, note 2; *CT*, vol. V, p. 18, note 5, and p. 19, note 1. The same attitude to Nacchianti as appears here is reflected in Massarelli's remark (vol. I, p. 494, line 18) calling him "novarum rerum cupidus", and in his report (vol. I, p. 494, line 22): "Reprehensus est a multis". The importance that Geiselmann attributes to him appears quite unconvincing in these circumstances, even apart from the other well-known grounds, which need not be repeated here.